Mug Hugs and Coaster Sets

Wake up your morning routine with playful mug hugs, or set a pretty table for afternoon guests with cheery coasters and placemats. The fun and practical designs in this collection feature some of the most popular Red Heart® yarns (Super Saver®, Soft®, and Gumdrop®). Feel free to choose your favorite colors from the dozens of options that are available.

I0867348

About Red Heart® Yarns

Red Heart is one of the most trusted brands in yarn. For over 75 years more people have chosen to make American heirlooms using Red Heart yarn than any other yarn. Red Heart yarns stand for quality, largest color selection, fashion and above all else, crafted with love. Whatever your creativity calls for, you'll find it in the Red Heart family.

LEISURE ARTS, INC.
Maumelle, Arkansas

Puppy Mug Hug

Designed by Michele Wilcox.

EASY

Mug Hug fits a mug that is 4" (10 cm) high with a 3" (7.5 cm) top diameter and a 2" (5 cm) bottom diameter.

SHOPPING LIST

Yarn (Medium Weight)

MEDIUM 4

RED HEART® Super Saver®:

- ☐ 360 Café Latte **A** - 1 skein
- ☐ 312 Black **B** - 1 skein
- ☐ 316 Soft White **C** - 1 skein

Crochet Hooks

- ☐ 3.5 mm [US E-4]
- ☐ 5 mm [US H-8]

Additional Supplies

- ☐ Yarn needle
- ☐ ¾" (19 mm) Button
- ☐ 5/16" (9 mm) Buttons for eyes - 2
- ☐ Black embroidery floss

GAUGE INFORMATION

12 sts and 12 rows = 3" (7.5 cm). **CHECK YOUR GAUGE.**

Use any size hook to obtain the specified gauge.

SPECIAL STITCH

sc2tog (single crochet 2 together): [Insert hook in next st, yo and pull up a loop] twice, yo and draw through all 3 loops on hook.

Note: Mug Hug size can be easily changed by adding or subtracting chains at beginning of Wrap and by adding or subtracting rows at end of Wrap.

MUG HUG

Wrap

With **A** and H hook, ch 14.

Row 1: Sc in 2nd ch from hook and in each ch across — 13 sc.

Rows 2-34: Ch 1, turn; working in back loops only *(Fig. 3, page 47)*, sc in each sc across. At end of Row 34, ch 10, slip st in last sc made on Row 34 (button loop made).
Fasten off.

Muzzle

With **C** and E hook, ch 2.

Round 1: 6 Sc in 2nd ch from hook — 6 sc.

Round 2: 2 Sc in each sc around — 12 sc.

Round 3: [Sc in next sc, 2 sc in next sc] around — 18 sc.

Round 4: [Sc in next 2 sc, 2 sc in next sc] around — 24 sc.
Fasten off.

Ear (Make 2)

With **B** and E hook, ch 5.

Row 1: Sc in 2nd ch from hook and in each ch across — 4 sc.

Row 2: Ch 1, turn; sc in first sc, 2 sc in each of next 2 sc, sc in last sc — 6 sc.

Rows 3-7: Ch 1, turn; sc in each sc across.

Row 8: Ch 1, turn; sc2tog, sc in next 2 sc, sc2tog — 4 sc.

Row 9: Ch 1, turn; [sc2tog] 2 times — 2 sc.

Row 10: Ch 1, turn; sc2tog. Fasten off.

Assembly

Using photo as a guide, page 3, embroider satin stitch nose *(Fig. A)* and straight stitch mouth *(Fig. B)* onto Muzzle with floss. Using **C**, sew Muzzle onto Wrap. With floss, sew 5/16" (9 mm) button eyes and Ears onto wrap. Sew ¾" (19 mm) button to beginning edge to correspond to button loop. Weave in ends.

Fig. A

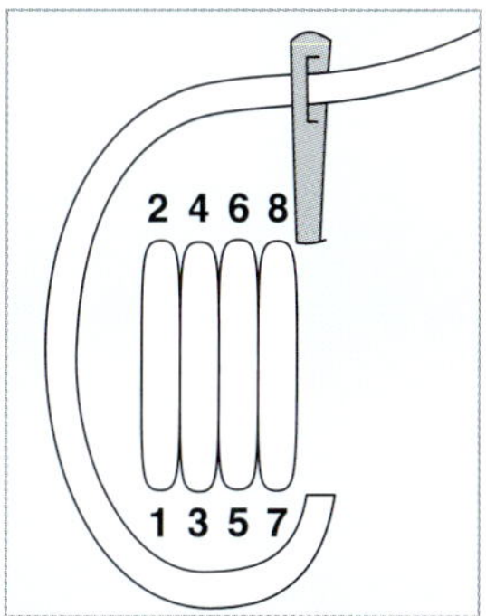

Fig. B

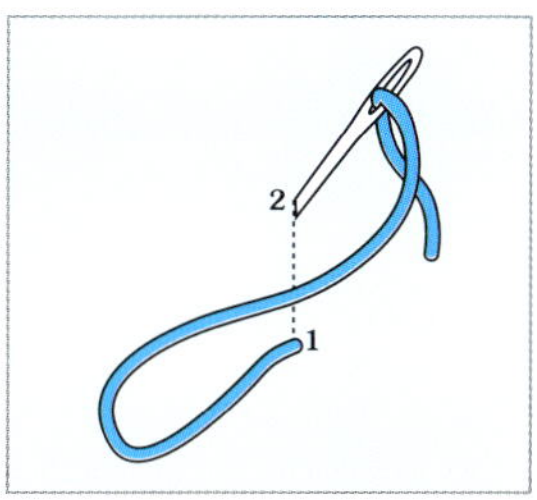

GOOD MORNING MUG HUG

Designed by Michele Wilcox.

EASY

Mug Hug fits a mug that is 4" (10 cm) high with a 3" (7.5 cm) top diameter and a 2" (5 cm) bottom diameter.

SHOPPING LIST

Yarn (Medium Weight)

MEDIUM 4

RED HEART® Super Saver®:

- ☐ 885 Delft Blue **A** - 1 skein
- ☐ 321 Gold **B** - 1 skein
- ☐ 312 Black **C** - 1 skein

Crochet Hook

- ☐ 5 mm [US H-8]

Additional Supplies

- ☐ Yarn needle
- ☐ ¾" (19 mm) Button
- ☐ Black embroidery floss

GAUGE INFORMATION

12 sc and 12 rows = 3" (7.5 cm). **CHECK YOUR GAUGE.**

Use any size hook to obtain the specified gauge.

Note: Mug Hug size can be easily changed by adding or subtracting chains at beginning of Wrap and by adding or subtracting rows at end of Wrap.

MUG HUG

Wrap

With **A**, ch 14.

Row 1: Sc in 2nd ch from hook and in each ch across — 13 sc.

Rows 2-40: Ch 1, turn; sc in each sc across. At end of Row 40, ch 10, slip st in last sc made on Row 40 (button loop made).
Fasten off.

Sew bottom 3 sts of beginning ch to bottom 3 sts of Row 40.

Sun

With **B**, ch 2.

Round 1: 6 Sc in 2nd ch from hook — 6 sc.

Round 2: 2 Sc in each sc around — 12 sc.

Round 3: [Sc in next sc, 2 sc in next sc] around — 18 sc.

Round 4: [Sc in next 2 sc, 2 sc in next sc] around — 24 sc.

Round 5: *Ch 4, slip st in 2nd ch from hook, hdc in next ch, dc in next ch, skip next 2 sc, slip st in next sc; repeat from * around.
Fasten off.

Nose

With **B**, ch 3; work 4 hdc in 3rd ch from hook. Fasten off.

Sunglasses (Make 2)

With **C**, ch 2; work 6 sc in 2nd ch from hook; join with slip st to first sc.
Fasten off.

Assembly

Using photo as a guide, fold nose in half lengthwise and sew onto sun with **B**. Using floss, sew sunglasses onto sun; embroider sides and middle of glasses with straight sts *(Fig. A)*; embroider couched stitch smile *(Figs. B-D)*. Using **B**, sew sun onto wrap. Sew button to beginning edge to correspond to button loop. Weave in yarn ends.

Fig. A

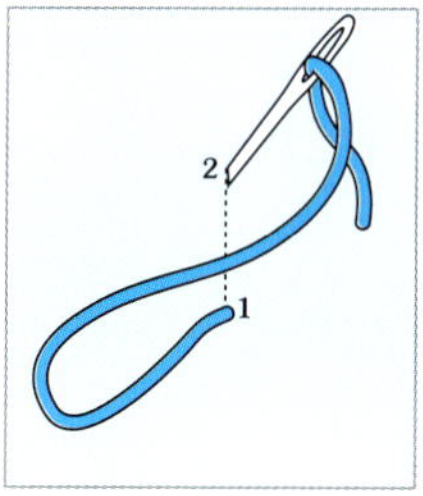

Fig. B

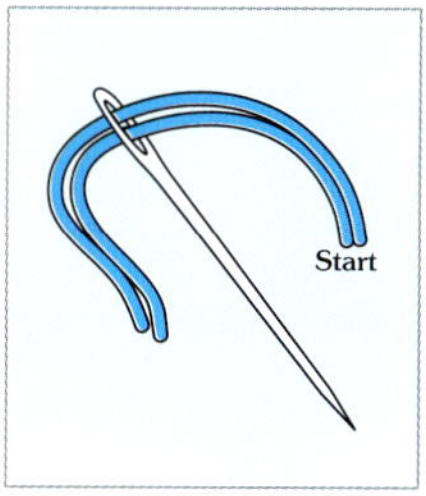

Fig. C

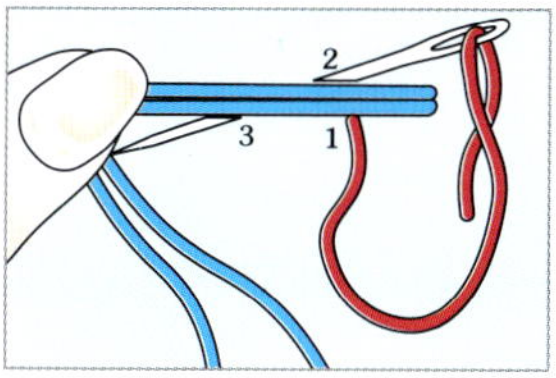

Fig. D

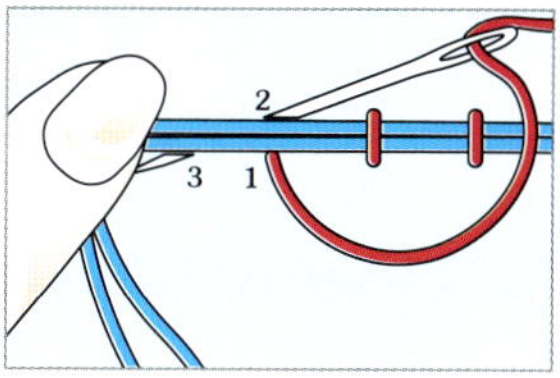

OWL Mug Hug

Designed by Michele Wilcox.

EASY

Mug Hug fits a mug that is 4" (10 cm) high with a 3½" (9 cm) diameter.

SHOPPING LIST

Yarn (Medium Weight) MEDIUM 4

RED HEART® Super Saver®:

- ☐ 944 Cherrycola **A** - 1 skein
- ☐ 321 Gold **B** - 1 skein
- ☐ 316 Soft White **C** - 1 skein

Crochet Hook

- ☐ 5 mm [US H-8]

Additional Supplies

- ☐ Yarn needle
- ☐ ¾" (19 mm) Wooden button
- ☐ ½" (12 mm) Buttons for eyes - 2

GAUGE INFORMATION

10 sts = 3" (7.5 cm); 8 rows = 3½" (9 cm) in pattern.

CHECK YOUR GAUGE. Use any size hook to obtain the specified gauge.

Note: Mug Hug size can be easily changed to fit any mug: To fit a taller or shorter mug, add or subtract an even number of chains at beginning of Wrap; to fit a wider or narrower mug, add or subtract an even number of rows.

MUG HUG

Wrap

With **A**, ch 14.

Row 1 (Wrong side): Sc in 2nd ch from hook and in each ch across — 13 sc.

Row 2 (Right side): Ch 3, turn; skip first st, dc in next st and in each st across.

Row 3: Ch 1, turn; slip st in first dc, *dc in next dc, slip st in next dc; repeat from * across working last slip st in top of ch-3.

Rows 4-23: Repeat Rows 2 and 3, 10 times.

Row 24: Ch 3, turn; skip first st, dc in next st and in each st across, ch 10, slip st in last dc made (button loop made).

Fasten off.

Beak

With **B**, ch 6; dc in 3rd ch from hook, hdc in next ch, sc in next ch, slip st in last ch.

Fasten off.

Eye (Make 2)

With **C**, ch 3; work 11 dc in 3rd ch from hook; join with slip st to top of ch-3.

Fasten off.

Sew ½" (12 mm) button to center of eye.

Finishing

Sew Beak and Eyes in place.

Sew ¾" (19 mm) button to beginning edge to correspond to button loop. Sew first 3 sts of Row 24 to corresponding 3 sts of beginning ch.

Weave in ends.

MUSTACHE MUG HUG

Designed by Michele Wilcox.

EASY

Mug Hug fits a mug that is 4" (10 cm) high with a 3½" (9 cm) diameter.

Shown on page 15.

SHOPPING LIST

Yarn (Medium Weight) MEDIUM 4

RED HEART® Super Saver®:

- ☐ 316 Soft White **A** - 1 skein
- ☐ 312 Black **B** - small amount

Crochet Hook

- ☐ 5 mm [US H-8]

Additional Supplies

- ☐ Yarn needle
- ☐ ¾" (19 mm) Button

GAUGE INFORMATION

16 sts = 4" (10 cm); 8 rows = 3" (7.5 cm). **CHECK YOUR GAUGE.**

Use any size hook to obtain the specified gauge.

SPECIAL STITCH

sc2tog (single crochet 2 together): [Insert hook in next st, yo and pull up a loop] twice, yo and draw through all 3 loops on hook.

MUG HUG

Wrap

With **A**, ch 13.

Row 1: Sc in 2nd ch from hook and in each ch across — 12 sc.

Rows 2-35: Ch 1, turn; sc in back loop only of each sc across ***(Fig. 3, page 47)***.

Row 36: Ch 8, turn; skip 8 chs, sc in back loop only of each sc across. Do **not** fasten off.

Bottom Shaping

Note: Remainder of Wrap is worked in rounds without turning.

Round 1: Continuing down side edge, work a sc in the end of each row; join with slip st to first sc — 36 sc.

Round 2: Ch 1, sc in same st as joining, sc2tog, *sc in next sc, sc2tog; repeat from * around; join with slip st to first sc — 24 sc. Fasten off.

Mustache

With **B**, ch 16.

Row 1: Slip st in 2nd ch from hook, pull up a loop in each of next 3 chs, yo and draw through all 4 loops on hook, hdc in next 2 chs, (dc, sc) in next ch, slip st in next ch, (sc, dc) in next ch, hdc in next 2 chs, pull up a loop in each of next 3 chs, yo and draw through all 4 loops on hook, slip st in last ch.
Fasten off.

Finishing

Referring to photo for placement, sew Mustache onto front of Wrap.

Sew button to beginning edge to correspond to button loop.

Weave in ends.

VALENTINE HEART COASTER

Designed by Andee Graves.

EASY

Each Coaster is 5" wide x 5¼" tall (12.5 cm x 13.5 cm).

SHOPPING LIST

Yarn (Medium Weight)

MEDIUM 4

RED HEART® Super Saver®:

- ☐ 319 Cherry Red - 1 skein
- ☐ 706 Perfect Pink - 1 skein

Crochet Hook

- ☐ 5 mm [US H-8]

Additional Supplies

- ☐ Stitch markers
- ☐ Yarn needle

GAUGE INFORMATION

8 sc and 8 rows = 2" (5 cm). **CHECK YOUR GAUGE.**

Use any size hook to obtain the specified gauge.

SPECIAL STITCH

reverse sc (reverse single crochet): Without turning work, insert hook in st to right of hook *(Fig. A)*, yo and pull up a loop *(Fig. B)*, yo and draw through both loops on hook *(Fig. C)* **(reverse sc made,** ***Fig. D)***.

Fig. A

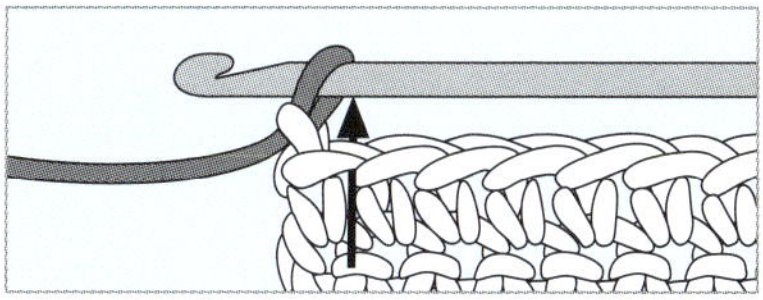

Fig. B

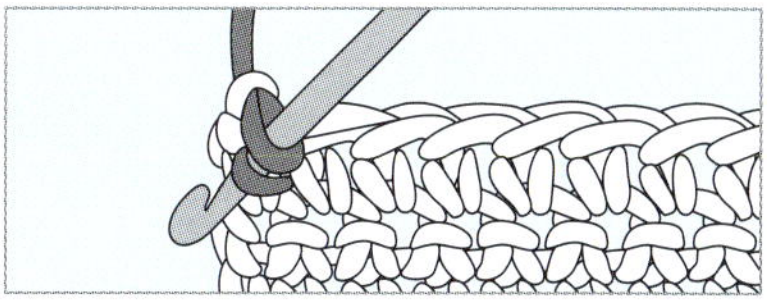

Fig. C

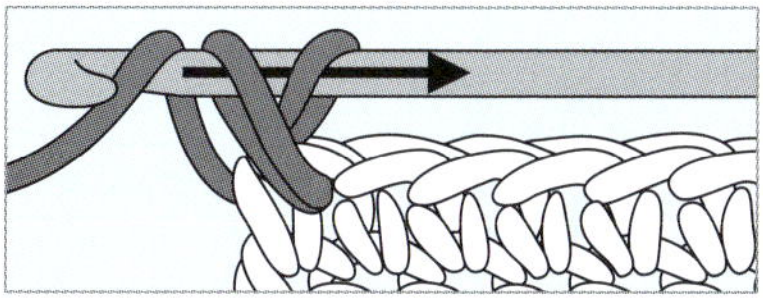

Fig. D

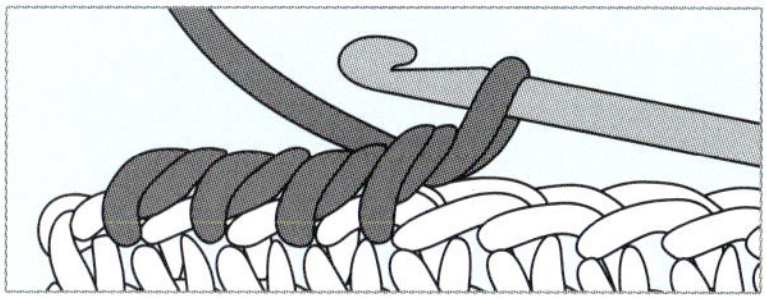

COASTER

(Make 1 in each color)

Note: Place marker in center ch-2 space of mitered square moving up to new ch-2 space as each row is completed.

Mitered Square

Row 1 (Right side): Ch 2, (sc, ch 2, sc) in 2nd ch from hook, place marker in ch-2 space — 2 sc and 1 ch-2 space.

Row 2: Ch 1, turn; sc in first sc, (sc, ch 2, sc) in marked ch-2 space, sc in last sc — 4 sc and 1 ch-2 space.

Rows 3-10: Ch 1, turn; sc in each sc across to marked ch-2 space, (sc, ch 2, sc) in marked ch-2 space, sc in each remaining sc across — 20 sc and 1 ch-2 space at end of last row.

First Hump

Row 1 (Right side): Ch 1, turn; sc in first 3 sc, skip next 2 sc, 5 dc in next sc, skip next 2 sc, sc in next 2 sc, sc in ch-2 sp — 6 sc and 5 dc.

Row 2: Turn; skip first 3 sc, 2 dc in each of next 2 dc, 3 dc in next dc, 2 dc in each of next 2 dc, skip next 2 sc, slip st in next sc — 11 dc. Fasten off.

Second Hump

Row 1: With right side facing, join yarn with sc in marked ch-2 space *(see Joining With Sc, page 44)*; sc in next 2 sc, skip next 2 sc, 5 dc in next sc, skip next 2 sc, sc in last 3 sc — 6 sc and 5 dc.

Row 2: Turn; skip first 3 sc, 2 dc in each of next 2 dc, 3 dc in next dc, 2 dc in each of next 2 dc, skip next 2 sc, slip st in next sc — 11 dc. Do **not** fasten off.

Edging

Row 1: Ch 1, turn; skip first slip st, 2 sc in next dc, [sc in next 2 dc, 2 sc in next dc] 3 times, sc in end of next 11 rows, (sc, ch 2, sc) in beginning ch at point *(Fig. 2, page 47)*, turn 90 degrees to work along next side, sc in end of next 11 rows, skip next slip st, 2 sc in next dc, [sc in next 2 dc, 2 sc in next dc] 3 times, ch 1, skip next dc, slip st in end of Row 1 of First Hump — 52 sc and 1 ch-2 space.

Row 2: Ch 1, do **not** turn; working from **left** to **right**, skip first slip st, reverse sc in next sc and in each sc around to ch space, reverse sc in ch space, reverse sc in next sc and in each remaining sc around, ch 1, slip st in end of Row 1 of Second Hump — 53 reverse sc. Fasten off.

Finishing

Weave in ends.

SNOWFLAKE COASTERS

Designed by Nancy Anderson.

EASY

Each Coaster is 3½" (9 cm) diameter.

SHOPPING LIST

Yarn (Medium Weight)

MEDIUM 4

RED HEART® Super Saver®:

- ☐ 505 Aruba Sea **A** - 1 skein
- ☐ 316 Soft White **B** - 1 skein
- ☐ 319 Cherry Red **C** - 1 skein

Crochet Hook

- ☐ 4 mm [US G-6]

Additional Supplies

- ☐ Yarn needle
- ☐ Spray starch (optional)

GAUGE INFORMATION

Each Coaster = 3½" (9 cm) diameter. **CHECK YOUR GAUGE. Use any size hook to obtain the specified gauge.**

COASTER

With desired color, make an adjustable loop *(Figs. 1a-d, page 46)*.

Round 1: Ch 1, 6 sc in loop; join with slip st to first sc — 6 sc.

Round 2: Ch 1, 2 sc in same st as joining and in each sc around; join with slip st to first sc — 12 sc.

Round 3: Ch 1, sc in same st as joining, 2 sc in next sc, ch 3, *sc in next sc, 2 sc in next sc, ch 3; repeat from * around; join with slip st to first sc — 18 sc and 6 ch-3 sps.

Round 4: Ch 1, sc in same st as joining and in next sc, skip next sc, (sc, ch 3, sc) in next ch-3 space, *skip next sc, sc in each of next 2 sc, (sc, ch 3, sc) in next ch-3 sp; repeat from * around; join with slip st to first sc — 24 sc and 6 ch-3 spaces.

Round 5: Ch 1, sc in same st as joining and in each of next 2 sc, slip st in next ch-3 space, [ch 4, hdc in 2nd ch from hook and in each of next 2 chs, slip st in same ch-3 space] twice, *skip next sc, sc in each of next 3 sc, slip st in next ch-3 space, [ch 4, hdc in 2nd ch from hook and in each of next 2 chs, slip st in same ch-3 space] twice; repeat from * around; join with slip st to first sc. Fasten off.

Repeat using colors **A**, **B** and **C** for desired number of Coasters.

Finishing

Weave in ends. Wet finished Coaster, flatten & straighten snowflake spokes, allow to dry.

For extra flattening, cover damp motif with waxed paper and place a heavy book on top until motif is dry.

Optional: Spray with laundry starch to stiffen as desired.

GRANNY SQUARE COASTER

BEGINNER

Each Coaster is 4" (10 cm) square.

Shown on page 25.

SHOPPING LIST

Yarn (Medium Weight) MEDIUM 4

RED HEART® Gumdrop®:

- ☐ 620 Cherry **A** - 1 skein

RED HEART® Soft®:

- ☐ 2515 Turquoise **B** - 1 skein
- ☐ 9528 Lilac **C** - 1 skein

Crochet Hook

- ☐ 4 mm [US G-6]

Additional Supplies

- ☐ Yarn needle

GAUGE INFORMATION

Finished Square = 4" (10 cm) square. **CHECK YOUR GAUGE.**

Use any size hook to obtain the specified gauge.

Color Sequence

Coaster #1

Rounds 1-4: **B**.

Coaster #2

Rounds 1 and 2: **A**.

Rounds 3 and 4: **B**.

Coaster #3

Rounds 1 and 2: **A**.

Rounds 3 and 4: **C**.

COASTER

With first color, ch 4; slip st in first ch to form a ring.

Round 1 (Right side): Ch 3 **(counts as dc here and throughout)**, 2 dc in ring, ch 3, *3 dc in ring, ch 3; repeat from * twice; join with slip st to top of beginning ch-3 — 12 dc and 4 ch-3 spaces. Fasten off.

Round 2: Slip st in next 2 dc and in next ch-3 space, ch 3, (2 dc, ch 3, 3 dc) in same ch-3 space, *(3 dc, ch 3, 3 dc) in next ch-3 space; repeat from * twice; join with slip st to top of beginning ch-3. Fasten off if changing color.

Round 3: Slip st in next 2 dc and in next corner ch-3 space **or** join next color with slip st in any corner ch-3 space; ch 3, (2 dc, ch 3, 3 dc) in same ch-3 space, *3 dc between next two 3-dc groups *(Fig. 4, page 47)***, (3 dc, ch 3, 3 dc) in next corner ch-3 space; repeat from * around, ending last repeat at **; join with slip st to top of beginning ch-3.

Round 4: Slip st in next 2 dc and in next ch-3 space, ch 3, (2 dc, ch 3, 3 dc) in same ch-3 space, *[3 dc between next two 3-dc groups] twice**, (3 dc, ch 3, 3 dc) in next corner ch-3 space; repeat from * around, ending last repeat at **; join with slip st to top of beginning ch-3. Fasten off.

Finishing

Weave in ends.

TASSELED COASTER

Designed by Kim Kotary.

BEGINNER

Each Coaster is 4" (10 cm) square, excluding tassels.

SHOPPING LIST

Yarn (Medium Weight)

MEDIUM 4

RED HEART® Super Saver®:

- ☐ 368 Paddy Green, 321 Gold **or** 376 Burgundy - 1 skein

Crochet Hook

- ☐ 5.5 mm [US I-9]

Additional Supplies

- ☐ Yarn needle
- ☐ ½" (12 mm) Bead - 4 per Coaster

GAUGE INFORMATION

12 sc and 15 rows = 4" (10 cm). **CHECK YOUR GAUGE.**

Use any size hook to obtain the specified gauge.

COASTER

Ch 13.

Row 1: Sc in 4th ch from hook, dc in next ch, [sc in next ch, dc in next ch] 4 times.

Row 2: Ch 3, turn; sc in next sc, [dc in next dc, sc in next sc] 4 times, dc in top of beginning ch.

Repeat Row 2 until piece measures 3" (7.5 cm) from beginning.

Edging Round: Ch 3 **(counts as hdc and ch 1)**, turn; skip next sc, [hdc in next dc, ch 1, skip next sc] 4 times, (hdc, ch 3, slip st in 2nd ch from hook, ch 1, hdc) all in top of beginning ch, turn to work along side edge, ch 1, [hdc, ch 1] 4 times evenly spaced along edge, turn to work on opposite side of foundation ch *(Fig. 2, page 47)*, (hdc, ch 3, slip st in 2nd ch from hook, ch 1, hdc) all in first st, ch 1, skip next ch, [hdc in next ch, ch 1, skip next ch] 4 times, (hdc, ch 3, slip st in 2nd ch from hook, ch 1, hdc) all in next ch, turn to work along side edge, ch 1, [hdc, ch 1] 4 times evenly spaced along edge, hdc in same st as beginning ch, ch 3, slip st in 2nd ch from hook, ch 1; join with slip st to 2nd ch of beginning ch. Fasten off.

Finishing

Weave in ends.

For corner tassels, thread two strands of yarn into yarn needle. Insert into corner, thread all four ends through bead, knot ends close to bead. Trim ends.

americana PLace SeTTiNg

Designed by Marilyn Coleman.

EASY

Placemat measures 13½" high x 18" wide (34.5 cm x 45.5 cm).

Coaster measures 6" (15 cm) across.

Napkin ring measures 4¾" (12 cm) circumference.

SHOPPiNg LiST

Yarn (Medium Weight) MEDIUM 4

RED HEART® Super Saver®:

Amount for 2 sets including placemat, coaster & napkin ring

- ☐ 319 Cherry Red **A** - 1 skein
- ☐ 316 Soft White **B** - 1 skein
- ☐ 387 Soft Navy **C** - 1 skein

Crochet Hook

- ☐ 4 mm [US G-6]

Additional Supplies

- ☐ Yarn needle

GAUGE INFORMATION

15 dc and 9 rows = 4" (10 cm). **CHECK YOUR GAUGE.**

Use any size hook to obtain the specified gauge.

AMERICANA SET

Placemat

With **A**, ch 58.

Row 1 (Right side): Dc in 4th ch from hook and in each ch across, changing to **B** in last dc *(Fig. A)* — 56 sts.

Fig. A

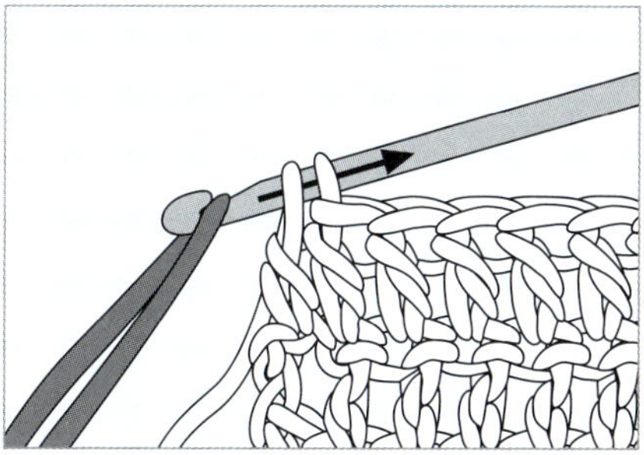

Row 2: With **B**, ch 3, turn; skip first dc, dc in next dc and in each dc across, dc in top of ch-3.

Repeat Row 2 and work stripe pattern of 1 more row **B**, then [2 rows **A**, 2 rows **B**] 4 times, then 1 more row **A**, changing to **C** in last dc of last row. Cut **A** and **B**.

Border

Round 1: With **C**, ch 1, turn; work sc evenly around all 4 sides, working 3 sc in each corner; join with slip st to first sc.

Round 2: Ch 3, do **not** turn; skip same st as joining, dc in each sc around, working 5 dc in center sc of each 3-sc corner group; join with slip st to top of ch-3.

Round 3: Ch 1, sc in same st as joining and in each dc around, working 3 sc in center dc of each 5-dc corner group; join with slip st to first sc.

Rounds 4-7: Repeat Rounds 2 and 3 twice more, changing to **A** in last sc of Round 7.

Round 8: With **A**, ch 1; sc in same st as joining and in each sc around; join with slip st to first sc. Fasten off.

Star (Make 4)

With **B**, ch 2; sc in 2nd ch from hook, *ch 3, slip st in 2nd ch from hook, sc in next ch**, sc in same ch as first sc*; repeat from * to * 3 more times, then from * to ** once more; join with slip st to first sc — 5 points.

Fasten off, leaving a long end for sewing.

Sew 1 star in each corner.

Weave in ends.

Coaster

Round 1: With **B**, ch 4; 14 dc in 4th ch from hook; join with slip st to top of ch-4 changing to **C** ***(Fig. B)*** — 15 sts.

Fig. B

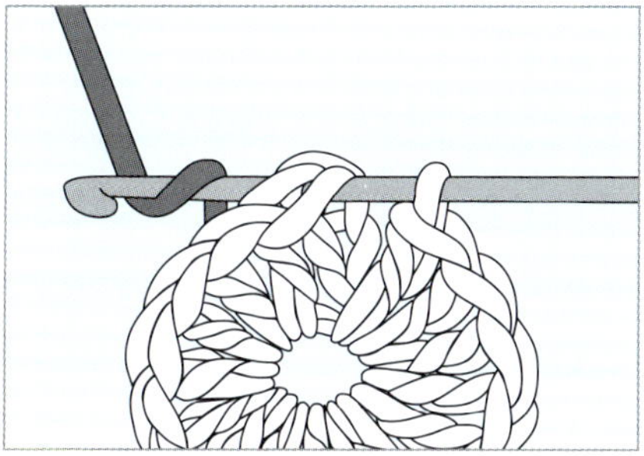

Round 2: With **C**, ch 3; working over **B**, 4 dc in same st as joining, changing to **B** in last dc made; *_with **B** and working over **C**, [insert hook in next st, yo and pull up a loop, yo and draw through 2 loops on hook] twice; with **C**, yo and draw through all 3 loops on hook_ – **cluster made****; with **C** and working over **B**, 5 dc in next dc changing to **B** in last dc made; repeat from * around, end at **; join with slip st to top of ch-3 — 30 sts. Cut **B**.

Round 3: With **C**, ch 3; dc in same st as joining, [dc in next dc, 2 dc in next dc] twice, *yo, insert hook from front to back to front around post of next cluster **(Fig. C)**, yo and pull up a loop, [yo and draw through 2 loops on hook] twice* – **front post dc (fpdc) made**, *2 dc in next dc, [dc in next dc, 2 dc in next dc] twice, fpdc; repeat from * around; join with slip st to top of ch-3 — 45 sts.

Fig. C

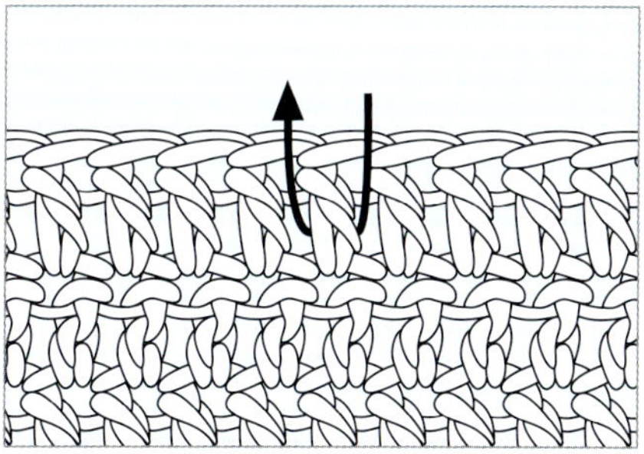

Round 4: Ch 3, dc in same st as joining, dc in next 2 sts, *2 dc in next st, dc in next 2 sts; repeat from * around; join with slip st to top of ch-3 — 60 dc.

Round 5: Ch 3, dc in same st as joining, dc in next 3 dc, *2 dc in next dc, dc in next 3 dc; repeat from * around, changing to **A** in last dc; join with slip st to top of ch-3 — 75 dc. Cut **C**.

Round 6: With **A**, ch 1; sc in each st around; join with slip st to first sc. Fasten off.
Weave in ends.

Napkin Ring

With **C**, ch 18; join with slip st to first ch to form a ring, taking care not to twist ch.

Round 1 (Right side): Ch 1, sc in each ch around; join with slip st to first sc.

Round 2: Ch 3, skip same st as joining, dc in next sc and in each sc around; join with slip st to top of ch-3.

Round 3: Ch 1, sc in same st as joining and in each dc around; join with slip st to first sc changing to **A**.

Round 4: With **A**, ch 1; sc in each sc around; join with slip st to first sc. Fasten off.

With right side facing and working in opposite side of beginning ch ***(Fig. 2, page 47)***, join **A** with slip st in any ch; ch 1, sc in same st as joining and in each ch around; join with slip st to first sc.
Fasten off.
Weave in ends.

With **B**, make 1 star same as for Placemat and sew to Napkin Ring.

STRIPED PLACEMAT

Designed by Vicki Blizzard.

EASY

Placemat measures 19" wide x 14" high (48.5 cm x 35.5 cm), excluding fringe.

Shown on page 35.

SHOPPING LIST

Yarn (Medium Weight) MEDIUM 4

RED HEART® Super Saver®:

Amount for one Placemat

- ☐ 376 Burgundy **A** - 1½ ounces
- ☐ 365 Coffee **B** - 1¼ ounces
- ☐ 661 Frosty Green **C** - 1 ounce
- ☐ 313 Aran **D** - 1 ounce
- ☐ 334 Buff **E** - 1 ounce

Crochet Hook

- ☐ 5.5 mm [US I-9]

Additional Supplies

- ☐ Yarn needle
- ☐ Liquid seam sealant (optional)

GAUGE INFORMATION

17 sts and 16 rows = 4" (10 cm) in pattern. **CHECK YOUR GAUGE. Use any size hook to obtain the specified gauge.**

PLACEMAT

Foundation Ch: With **A**, ch 95. Fasten off.

Row 1 (Right side): With **A**, ch 7 for fringe, sc in 8th ch of foundation ch, *ch 1, skip next ch, sc in next ch; repeat from * across until 7 chs remain on foundation ch, do **not** work into these chs, ch 7 for fringe. Fasten off.

Row 2: With **A**, ch 7 for fringe, sc in first sc, *ch 1, skip next ch-1 space, sc in next sc; repeat from * across, ch 7 for fringe. Fasten off.

Rows 3-55: Repeat Row 2 in the following color sequence:

2 rows **B**
1 row **C**
1 row **D**
1 row **C**
2 rows **E**
1 row **A**
1 row **B**
1 row **A**
2 rows **C**
2 rows **B**
3 rows **A**
2 rows **B**
1 row **D**
1 row **C**
1 row **D**
2 rows **E**
3 rows **A**
2 rows **E**
1 row **D**
1 row **C**
1 row **D**
2 rows **B**
3 rows **A**
2 rows **B**
2 rows **C**
1 row **A**
1 row **B**
1 row **A**
2 rows **E**
1 row **C**
1 row **D**
1 row **C**
2 rows **B**
2 rows **A**.

Finishing

Weave in ends **OR** pull end of yarn on fringe to make sure knot is tight against ch; trim end close to knot. If desired, secure knot with a drop of seam sealant to prevent raveling.

OVAL PLACEMAT & COASTER

EASY

Placemat measures 14" high x 19" wide (35.5 cm x 48.5 cm).

Coaster measures 5½" (14 cm) across.

SHOPPING LIST

Yarn (Medium Weight) MEDIUM 4

RED HEART® Soft®:

Amount for one Set

☐ 4601 Off White **A** - 2 skeins

☐ 9388 Wheat **B** - 1 skein

Crochet Hook

☐ 5.5 mm [US I-9]

Additional Supplies

☐ Yarn needle

GAUGE INFORMATION

Placemat Rnd 1 = 6" long x 1¼" wide (15 cm x 3 cm).

CHECK YOUR GAUGE. Use any size hook to obtain the specified gauge.

OVAL SET

Placemat

With **A**, ch 19.

Round 1: 4 Dc in 4th ch from hook **(ch 3 counts as dc)**, dc in next 14 chs, 5 dc in last ch; working on opposite side of beginning ch *(Fig. 2, page 47)*, dc in next 14 chs; join with slip st to top of ch-3 — 38 dc.

Round 2: Ch 3, dc in same st as joining, 2 dc in each of next 4 dc, dc in next 14 dc, 2 dc in each of next 5 dc, dc in last 14 dc; join with slip st to top of ch-3 — 48 dc.

Round 3: Ch 3, dc in same st as joining, 2 dc in each of next 9 dc, dc in next 14 dc, 2 dc in each of next 10 dc, dc in last 14 dc; join with slip st to top of ch-3 — 68 dc.

Round 4: Ch 1, (sc, ch 4, sc) all in same st as joining, skip next dc, *(sc, ch 4, sc) all in next dc, skip next dc; repeat from * around; join with slip st to first sc — 34 ch-4 spaces.

Rounds 5-7: Slip st in next ch-4 space, ch 1, *(sc, ch 4, sc) all in same space and in each ch-4 space around; join with slip st to first sc.

Round 8: Slip st in next ch-4 space, ch 1, 3 sc in same space, *[ch 2, 3 sc in next ch-4 space] 9 times, ch 2, 2 sc in each of next 7 ch-4 spaces, ch 2**, 3 sc in next ch-4 space; repeat from * to ** once; join with slip st to first sc — 88 sc and 22 ch-2 spaces.

Round 9: Ch 3, skip same st as joining, dc in next 2 sc, *[3 dc in next ch-2 space, dc in next 3 sc] 9 times, 3 dc in next ch-2 space, dc in next 14 sc, 3 dc in next ch-2 space**, dc in next 3 sc; repeat from * to **; join with slip st to first sc — 154 dc.

Rounds 10 and 11: Ch 3, dc in each dc around; join with slip st to top of ch-3.

Fasten off.

Round 12: With right side facing, join **B** with slip st in same st as joining; ch 1, (sc, ch 4, sc) all in same st, skip next dc, *(sc, ch 4, sc) all in next dc, skip next dc; repeat from * around; join with slip st to first sc — 77 ch-4 spaces.

Rounds 13-15: Slip st in next ch-4 space, ch 1, *(sc, ch 4, sc) all in same space and in each ch-4 space around; join with slip st to first sc.

Fasten off.

Coaster

With **A**, ch 4.

Round 1: 11 Dc in 4th ch from hook; join with slip st to top of ch-4 — 12 sts.

Round 2: Ch 3, dc in same st as joining, 2 dc in each dc around; join with slip st to top of ch-3 — 24 dc.

Round 3: Ch 3, 2 dc in each of next 2 dc, *dc in next dc, 2 dc in each of next 2 dc; repeat from * around; join with slip st to top of ch-3 — 40 dc.
Fasten off.

Round 4: With right side facing, join **B** with slip st in same st as joining; ch 1, (sc, ch 4, sc) all in same st, skip next dc, *(sc, ch 4, sc) all in next dc, skip next dc; repeat from * around; join with slip st to first sc — 20 ch-4 spaces.

Round 5: Slip st in next ch-4 space, ch 1, *(sc, ch 4, sc) all in same space and in each ch-4 space around; join with slip st to first sc.
Fasten off.

Finishing

Weave in ends.

PiNWHeeLS FOr THe TaBLe

Designed by Mary Jane Protus.

INTERMEDIATE

Placemat measures approximately 16" (40.5 cm) across.

Coaster measures approximately 4½" (11.5 cm) across.

SHOPPiNg LiST

Yarn (Medium Weight)

MEDIUM 4

RED HEART® Super Saver®:

Amount will make a complete set of 4 placemats & 4 coasters, two in each color combination

- ☐ 319 Cherry Red **A** - 1 skein
- ☐ 316 Soft White **B** - 1 skein
- ☐ 368 Paddy Green **C** - 1 skein

Crochet Hook

- ☐ 5.5 mm [US I-9]

Additional Supplies

- ☐ Stitch marker
- ☐ Yarn needle

GAUGE INFORMATION

12 sc and 15 rows = 4" (10 cm).

Gauge is not crucial in this pattern.

Note: Instructions are written using **A** + **B** for spiral. Change colors for other color combinations.

PINWHEEL SET

Placemat

Center: With **A**, ch 4; join with slip st to first ch to form a ring; ch 1, (sc, hdc, 3 dc) all into ring, drop **A**, **DO NOT FASTEN OFF**; following the **A** sts, join **B** with a sc in ring ***(see Joining With Sc, page 44)***, work (hdc, 3 dc) all into same ring, drop **B**, **DO NOT FASTEN OFF**.

Round 1: Pick up **A**, work 2 dc into each **B** st — 10 dc **A**; drop **A**, pick up **B**, work 2 dc in each **A** st around — 30 dc **B**, drop **B**.

Round 2: Pick up **A**, *dc in next dc, 2 dc in next dc; repeat from * around — 45 dc **A**; drop **A**, pick up **B** and repeat from * to last st, dc in last st — 67 dc **B**, drop **B**.

Note: Piece may begin to ruffle beginning with the next round, but will lie flat when Placemat is completed.

Round 3: Pick up **A**, dc in next 3 dc, [2 dc in next dc, dc in next 3 dc] 16 times — 83 dc **A**; drop **A**, pick up **B**, dc in next 6 dc, [2 dc in next dc, dc in next 6 dc] 11 times — 94 dc **B**, drop **B**.

Round 4: Pick up **A**, [dc in next 10 dc, 2 dc in next dc] 8 times, dc in next 6 dc — 102 dc **A**; drop **A**, pick up **B**, [dc in next 6 dc, 2 dc in next dc] 14 times, dc in last 4 dc — 116 dc **B**, drop **B**.

Round 5: Pick up **A**, [dc in next 10 dc, 2 dc in next dc] 10 times, dc in next 6 dc — 126 dc **A**; drop **A**, pick up **B**, [dc in next 10 dc, 2 dc in next dc] 11 times, dc in last 5 dc — 137 dc **B**, drop **B**.

Round 6: Pick up **A**, [dc in next 14 dc, 2 dc in next dc] 9 times, dc in next 2 dc — 146 dc **A**; drop **A**, pick up **B**, [dc in next 18 dc, 2 dc in next dc] 7 times, dc in last 13 dc — 153 dc **B**. Mark 77th dc from hook.

Round 7: Pick up **A**, *dc in next 18 dc, 2 dc in next dc; repeat from * to marker, remove marker; **hdc in next 2 dc, sc in next dc, slip st in next dc**; fasten off **A**; pick up **B**; repeat from ** to ** across next 4 dc. Fasten off **B**.

BORDER

With right side facing, join **C** with slip st in any st; ch 1, (sc, ch 2, sc) in same st as joining, skip next st, *(sc, ch 2, sc) in next st, skip next st; repeat from * around; join with slip st to first sc. Fasten off. Weave in ends.

Coaster

Work same as Placemat through Round 1.

Round 2: Pick up **A**, 2 dc in next 10 dc, *dc in next dc, hdc in next dc, sc in next dc, slip st in next dc*; fasten off **A**, pick up **B**; repeat from * to * across next 4 dc. Fasten off **B**.

BORDER

With right side facing, join **C** with slip st in any st; ch 1, (sc, ch 2, sc) in same st as joining, skip next st, *(sc, ch 2, sc) in next st, skip next st; repeat from * around; join with slip st to first sc. Fasten off. Weave in ends.

general instructions

ABBREVIATIONS

ch(s)	chain(s)
cm	centimeters
dc	double crochet(s)
fpdc	front post double crochet(s)
hdc	half double crochet(s)
mm	millimeters
sc	single crochet(s)
sc2tog	single crochet 2 together
st(s)	stitch(es)
yo	yarn over

SYMBOLS & TERMS

( ) or [ ] = work directions in parentheses or brackets the number of times specified.

* **or** ** = repeat whatever follows the * or ** as indicated.

CROCHET TERMINOLOGY		
UNITED STATES		INTERNATIONAL
slip stitch (slip st)	=	single crochet (sc)
single crochet (sc)	=	double crochet (dc)
half double crochet (hdc)	=	half treble crochet (htr)
double crochet (dc)	=	treble crochet (tr)
treble crochet (tr)	=	double treble crochet (dtr)
double treble crochet (dtr)	=	triple treble crochet (ttr)
triple treble crochet (tr tr)	=	quadruple treble crochet (qtr)
skip	=	miss

GAUGE

Gauge refers to the number of stitches and rows in a given area. When making projects, ensure that your project is the correct finished size and is to gauge. Work the area as stated in the pattern and then measure to check that it agrees with the gauge given. If it is not the same size, change your hook size. If it is too large, use a smaller hook. If it is too small, use a larger hook.

JOINING WITH SC

When instructed to join with sc, begin with a slip knot on hook. Insert hook in stitch or space indicated, yo and pull up a loop, yo and draw through both loops on hook.

CROCHET HOOKS																	
U.S.	B-1	C-2	D-3	E-4	F-5	G-6	7	H-8	I-9	J-10	K-10½	L-11	M/N-13	N/P-15	P/Q	Q	S
Metric - mm	2.25	2.75	3.25	3.5	3.75	4	4.5	5	5.5	6	6.5	8	9	10	15	16	19

BEGINNER	Projects for first-time crocheters using basic stitches. Minimal shaping.
EASY	Projects using yarn with basic stitches, repetitive stitch patterns, simple color changes, and simple shaping and finishing.
INTERMEDIATE	Projects using a variety of techniques, such as basic lace patterns or color patterns, mid-level shaping and finishing.
EXPERIENCED	Projects with intricate stitch patterns, techniques and dimension, such as non-repeating patterns, multi-color techniques, fine threads, small hooks, detailed shaping and refined finishing.

Yarn Weight Symbol & Names	LACE 0	SUPER FINE 1	FINE 2	LIGHT 3	MEDIUM 4	BULKY 5	SUPER BULKY 6	JUMBO 7
Type of Yarns in Category	Fingering, size 10 crochet thread	Sock, Fingering, Baby	Sport, Baby	DK, Light Worsted	Worsted, Afghan, Aran	Chunky, Craft, Rug	Super Bulky, Roving	Jumbo, Roving
Crochet Gauge* Ranges in Single Crochet to 4" (10 cm)	32-42 sts**	21-32 sts	16-20 sts	12-17 sts	11-14 sts	8-11 sts	6-9 sts	5 sts and fewer
Advised Hook Size Range	Steel*** 6 to 8, Regular hook B-1	B-1 to E-4	E-4 to 7	7 to I-9	I-9 to K-10½	K-10½ to M/N-13	M/N-13 to Q	Q and larger

*GUIDELINES ONLY: The chart above reflects the most commonly used gauges and hook sizes for specific yarn categories.

** Lace weight yarns are usually crocheted with larger hooks to create lacy openwork patterns. Accordingly, a gauge range is difficult to determine. Always follow the gauge stated in your pattern.

*** Steel crochet hooks are sized differently from regular hooks–the higher the number, the smaller the hook, which is the reverse of regular hook sizing.

ADJUSTABLE LOOP

Wind yarn around two fingers to form a ring *(Fig. 1a)*. Slide the yarn off fingers and grasp the strands at the top of the ring *(Fig. 1b)*. Insert hook from **front** to **back** into the ring, pull up a loop, yo and draw through loop on hook to lock ring *(Fig. 1c)* (stitch made does **not** count as a beginning chain). Working around **both** strands, follow instructions to work stitches in the ring, then pull yarn tail to close *(Fig. 1d)*.

Fig. 1a

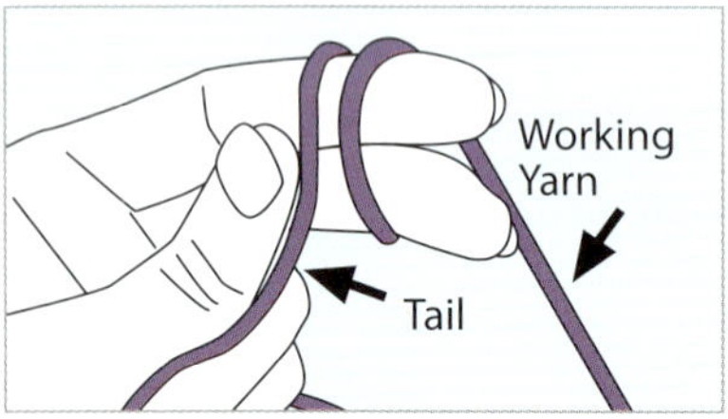

Fig. 1b

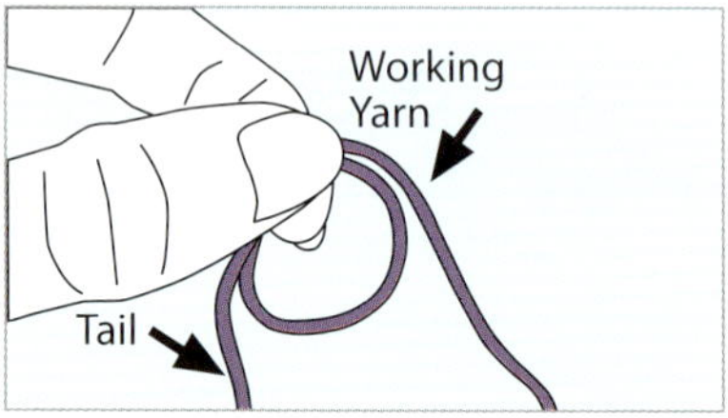

Fig. 1c

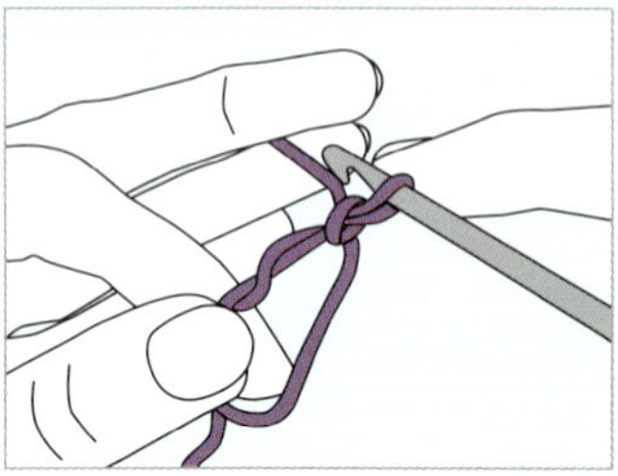

Fig. 1d

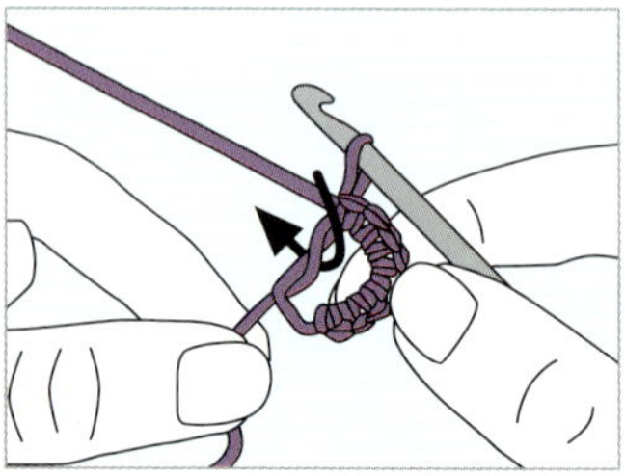

UNUSED LOOPS OF A CHAIN

When instructed to work in unused loops of a chain or opposite side of a chain, work in loop indicated by arrow *(Fig. 2)*.

Fig. 2

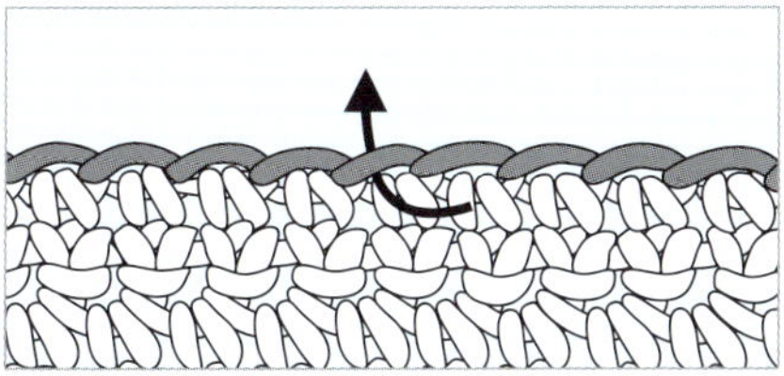

BACK LOOP ONLY

Work only in loop(s) indicated by arrow *(Fig. 3)*.

Fig. 3

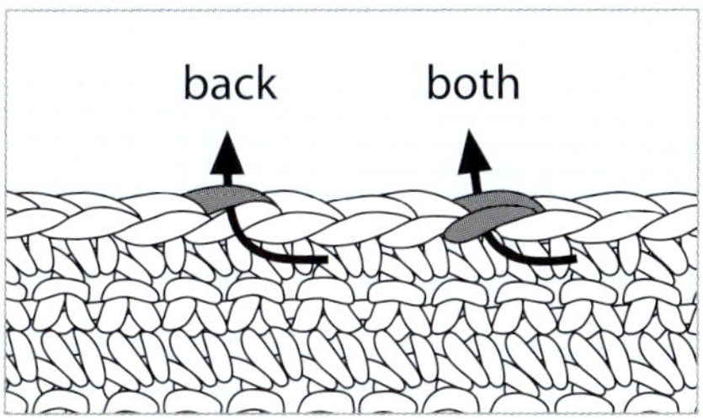

WORKING IN SPACE BETWEEN STITCHES

When instructed to work in a space between stitches, insert hook into space indicated by arrow *(Fig. 4)*.

Fig. 4

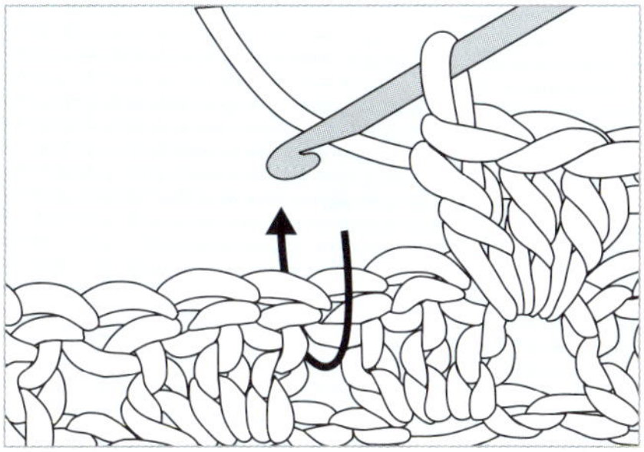

YARN INFORMATION

The projects in this book were created with **RED HEART®** yarns. For best results, we recommend following the pattern exactly as written. Be sure to purchase the amounts recommended in the pattern, and retain your labels. Always follow the care instructions provided on the label.

RED HEART® Super Saver®

MEDIUM 4

Art. E300 available in solid colors
7 oz (198 g), 364 yd (333 m);
in prints, multis & heathers 5 oz
(141 g), 244 yd (223 m); and in flecks
5 oz (141 g), 260 yd (238 m) skeins

RED HEART® Soft®

MEDIUM 4

Art. E728 available in solid colors
5 oz (141 g), 256 yd (234 m);
in prints 4 oz (113 g), 204 yd (187 m);
and in heathers 4 oz (113 g),
212 yd (194 m) balls.

RED HEART® Gumdrop®

MEDIUM 4

Art. E800 available in multicolor
4 oz (113 g),
204 yd (187 m) balls.

FOR MORE IDEAS & INSPIRATION

www.redheart.com • www.facebook.com/redheartyarns
www.pinterest.com/redheartyarns • www.twitter.com/redheartyarns
www.youtube.com/redheartyarns • Instagram@redheartyarns

We have made every effort to ensure that these instructions are accurate and complete. We cannot, however, be responsible for human error, typographical mistakes, or variations in individual work.